Not So Silent Night

Not So Silent Night

Written by: Kayce Clark
Cover Illustration by: Randall King

gatekeeper press™
Tampa, Florida

This book is a work of fiction. The names, characters and events in this book are the products of the author's imagination or are used fictitiously. Any similarity to real persons living or dead is coincidental and not intended by the author.

The views and opinions expressed in this book are solely those of the author and do not necessarily reflect the views or opinions of Gatekeeper Press. Gatekeeper Press is not to be held responsible for and expressly disclaims responsibility of the content herein.

Not So Silent Night

Published by Gatekeeper Press
7853 Gunn Hwy, Suite 209
Tampa, FL 33626
www.GatekeeperPress.com

Copyright © 2022 by Kayce Clark

All rights reserved. Neither this book, nor any parts within it may be sold or reproduced in any form or by any electronic or mechanical means, including information storage and retrieval systems, without permission in writing from the author. The only exception is by a reviewer, who may quote short excerpts in a review.

The cover design for this book is entirely the product of the author. Gatekeeper Press did not participate in and is not responsible for any aspect of this element.

Library of Congress Control Number: 2022948688

ISBN (paperback): 9781662933363

*Dedicated to my Mom, Janna, who keeps Christmas
in her heart all year long.*

Contents

PROLOGUE		3
1.	THE INNKEEPER	7
2.	THE INNKEEPER'S WIFE	13
3.	THE LITTLE BOY	19
4.	THE OLD SHEPHERD	23
5.	MARY	27
6.	JOSEPH	31
7.	GABRIEL	35
8.	JESUS	39
EPILOGUE: THE REAL SOUNDS OF CHRISTMAS		43

Prologue

Crash. There it was, I just knew it. The final member of my nativity set had bitten the dust.

This was now the fifth nativity set that had succumbed to the tiny tornadoes that were my three young sons. My boys seemed to think that our nativity set was a playset with really cool action figures, and we would find Joseph in my son's room battling Iron Man, or Mary and a wise man making the trek to the kitchen for a little gingersnap cookie.

Well, if you have sons or grandsons, you know that if three little boys are playing with any set that isn't made of titanium, it's going to break.

I had bought this latest nativity set just a month before at a Christmas market here in town. I have had to throw away four previous sets, and it sounded like the fifth was on its way to the trash can as well.

It's not that I didn't like these sets. On the contrary, each one was beautiful and each one, I thought, would be our forever nativity. I had dreams of my boys coming home from college or home for Christmas with their own young families and showing them our decades-old nativity set and telling their own children stories of seeing it displayed proudly in our home all the years they were growing up.

Well, that was clearly not going to happen. I walked into the living room and was not surprised to see the last wise man lying on the floor, headless. His crash to our hardwood floors marked a grand total of fifteen wise men, twenty-two shepherds, five Marys, five Josephs, and countless manger animals, all who found themselves without arms, legs, or heads.

For a while, I simply placed the armless Joseph, the headless wise man, or the sheep with only one leg and no head back on the table. I guess I hoped no one would notice, and at first they didn't.

One headless horseman in your nativity is one thing, but once every single member of the holy scene looked as if they'd been through a war, that was another. I eventually had to throw them away for new ones.

Each set I bought I thought was made of stronger stuff that could withstand life with three boys under age five...but it appeared even the strongest materials were no match for my crew.

And while I loved that story of my nativity set with no heads, and while it did make me crazy that I had to remind them that baby Jesus was just to look at and not to use as a submarine in the bathtub, I tried to remind myself that I also loved that they were playing with such a special representation of the truth of Christmas.

No, they weren't playing with them according to the real story, but it didn't matter. They were still playing with them in their own little-boy way. They were still putting down the iPad, setting aside the Superman toy, and were picking up baby Jesus.

So, as I swept up the last of this nativity and placed it in the trashcan, I reminded myself that as frustrating as it was, this nativity playtime was a playtime I could get behind. As I looked at the empty space where the nativity sat just minutes ago, I thought about how many times I had walked right past these nativity sets in our home or in the market or in the lobby of church.

I began to wonder, do we really consider that these aren't just playthings or toys or a pretty addition to our decorations that get packed up in January?

These are the depictions of real people, people who walked daily with our Lord. People who witnessed the most amazing story ever told. Were any of us really seeing it that way? Were any of us seeing the story behind the figures?

Students in school often will ask their grandparents what it was like to witness major events in history. "Where were you when you heard about Pearl Harbor?"

"What did you think when you heard JFK was shot?"

"How did it feel to see the Berlin Wall come down?"

"What was the heartache as you watched the Twin Towers collapse?"

These stories are fascinating because when we talk to someone who was there, who saw it, who heard it, who lived it, it becomes so much more than words on a page. It comes to life, much like these characters do when people pick them up and really look at them.

We tell our stories in books and in movies, in song and in pictures, but no matter how we tell our stories, they are always based on what we saw, felt, smelled, and heard.

As I sat on my floor and stared at the now empty table, I let my mind wander back to Bethlehem, back to the lives of the real-life people depicted in these figures. I wondered what it would have been like to talk a way through Bethlehem that night and to hear these people tell me their story.

Chapter 1
THE INNKEEPER

That was one hundred eleven. One hundred eleven knocks on his door just today.

The sound of that door pounding was still ringing in his ears. It was true, Harrod's decree that everyone return to their town of origin had done wonders for his business, but it was doing a number on his nerves.

The innkeeper in this small town of Bethlehem used to long for the sound of a knock on his door. That knock meant that a guest had arrived. He loved owning an inn. It allowed him to meet new people, to make them feel at home, and to welcome them to this little town he loved so much.

He had grown up in Bethlehem, and while many people saw it as a nothing, out-of-the-way, useless little town, he loved it here. He loved that he knew all of his neighbors, he loved that he was able to see the children of his friends grow up, and he loved that he was able to work in this inn that had been in his family for generations.

He grew up watching his father and grandfather welcome weary travelers into its warm rooms. He would listen to their stories, hear their many languages, and see their many traditions. He learned from his father the art of hospitality, of welcoming someone and making them feel at home.

He took this responsibility very seriously and nothing meant more to him than being a good innkeeper. He insisted on the rooms being clean and prepared at all times, ready to welcome any guest who arrived. He made sure there was always enough linen, enough food, enough drink, and enough warmth for anyone who needed him.

He had to be prepared. He had to supply everything these guests might need. It was his responsibility to ensure they had what they needed to enjoy themselves and to be comfortable. The sound of that door knocking had always alerted him that now was the time to jump to it, now was the time he was needed and must provide…and yet, now the sound of that door made his heart sink.

Thirty-three. Thirty-three guests resting upstairs.

His inn was made to hold twelve guests at a time and even that was tight, and being as prepared as he was, he always had supplies and food for as many as twenty guests, although he had never needed anywhere near that much.

But now the pantry was empty, the beds were full, and he had nothing left to give. He had spent his whole life wanting to serve others in his home, and yet now all he had was one phrase: "I'm sorry, there is no room."

That was all. He had nothing left to give. He simply did not have enough to give to the large amounts of visitors who knocked this night. He had run out of food, run out of linens, run out of beds. He had even pulled from the store house to squeeze the last bit of dinner he could for the last guest who had arrived. And that was merely a small jar of olives and a piece of salted fish.

He had untucked the heavy blanket his mother had made for him as a child and handed it over to a traveler who could only be given a place on the floor to sleep. A place on the floor! What would his father say if he could see his son, the innkeeper, placing guests on the floor? No matter what he did, there just wasn't enough.

He walked to the storehouse one more time, although he knew what he would find there, or rather what he wouldn't find there. He listened as the door creaked open and as his footsteps echoed in the empty room. Why had he not saved more? Why had he not prepared more? His ears burned with the silent accusation of not having enough.

Three times he walked the room, searching for one small piece of food or one small blanket that might have hidden itself somewhere in the darkness. But there was nothing there. There was nothing left to do but sit in his chair, wait for the next knock at his door, and sigh. So, he did it.

The more he sat and strained his ears to hear footsteps approaching, the more his heart filled with despair. He simply didn't have enough. He simply wasn't enough. This was the most important time in his life, a once-in-a-lifetime event, hundreds of people streaming into his beloved town, into his beloved inn, and yet he didn't have enough to go around.

While he looked around his home, he knew that he was blessed. He knew that he had given all that he had and part of him understood that he couldn't give everything to everyone, but that didn't help the ache in his heart.

He wanted to do more, he wanted to give more, he wanted to share, and yet he had nothing left to give. He sat in the quiet and just listened.

Listened for the door. He heard the crackle of the small fire that illuminated the room. He knew he should be grateful for its warmth and yet his mind focused on its small size; it just wasn't enough. He heard the snoring of a guest upstairs. He had filled every available space, even the open spaces on the floors, but it just wasn't enough.

He could hear the animals in the barn rustling about. How would he feed them, when he couldn't even provide enough food for his guests? There just wasn't enough. This week that should have been full of new friends, stories from old friends come home again, laughter, and welcome instead was just a reminder that he didn't have enough to give.

He was just about to turn in for the night when he heard it. There it was again, a knock on his door. Oh, his heart couldn't bear to tell one more person that he couldn't give them what they so desperately wanted. He loved people, he loved to give, and yet he prepared himself to say, once again, no.

He opened the door to find a young man standing there, clearly exhausted. The man was out of breath, and it was difficult to hear what he was saying over the panting. Finally, he understood that the man was looking for a place for himself and his wife for the night.

Once again, the inn keeper had no choice but to tell the man he had run out of space and food. The deflated sigh that escaped the young man's lips pierced the innkeeper's ears. This man seemed so much more disappointed and distressed than any of the others he had had to turn away that night. That's when he heard the next sound, the sound of a young woman.

He looked past the man to see a very pregnant, very young woman standing behind him. The innkeeper's heart sank further. So, not only could he not give these people what they wanted so badly, he now had to say no to a pregnant lady? He didn't think he could bear the disappointment in the young man's face.

As the man quietly thanked him and turned to go, the innkeeper heard the barn animals stirring again. He had an idea, although even the thought of it made his ears turn red-hot. Surely, he couldn't offer them the barn. To ask a young couple, and a pregnant woman at that, to sleep in a barn, how could he even bring himself to form the words? Is this what it had come to? All of his preparation, all of his desire to serve and to give and to help, and now he was offering up a smelly, dirty, humbling barn to these weary travelers.

It was all he had, so it was all he could offer. He was expecting to hear an insulted snarl or an amused laugh from the man when he mentioned the available barn, and yet what he heard was an enthusiastic and grateful "thank you."

How could that be? He stood in astonishment at the graciousness of this couple for a moment, and then he heard the young woman breathing heavily behind her husband. It was clear she needed to rest right away.

He grabbed a lantern and asked them to follow him up the path, behind the house, and to the barn. As he led the couple to the barn, he continued to be amazed at what he had heard behind him. The young couple was actually relieved. They kept talking to each other about the blessing of finding him and the availability of his barn. He couldn't believe his ears. They were thankful? For this?

Of all the guests he had settled in for the night, none had offered him such a sincere thank you. He had guests in large rooms with comfortable beds, guests with full bellies and warm blankets; and yet his biggest thank you came from his most humble offering he had to give. As he walked back to his inn, he pondered this sound, this gentle, humble, and truly grateful "thank you." It was not the large things he had given this night, but this small, almost insignificant thing that rang in his ears as he closed the door and blew out the light.

Chapter 2
THE INNKEEPER'S WIFE

She heard the door close, the candle blown out, and her husband head to sleep. She knew he had a lot on his mind and must be exhausted, but didn't he understand that just giving their guests a place to stay and a warm meal wasn't the end of the story?

Here she was up in the middle of the night, cleaning and preparing the inn for the next day. Nothing like this had ever happened to Bethlehem before, never before had there been this many people coming in and out of their inn, and it must look perfect. She had to be sure everything was spick and span, that the food looked beautiful and tasted delicious. She must ensure she looked her best and that the house was welcoming and the palace perfect.

This was no palace, she knew that, but she certainly could get it as close to royalty worthy as she could. Not only would newcomers and guests be coming in and out, but her friends and neighbors were sure to stop by to see the bustling inn at this special time.

What would they think if they found dirt on the floor, a rug askew, or trays of food left empty and unappealing? If her husband was concerned about having enough, she was more concerned with making what they did have look perfect.

She admired her husband for his generosity. She knew how much he loved to share and to give, and her heart also swelled when they saw the smile on guests' faces as they looked at a clean room to rest and a heaping pile of food to eat. She truly loved this opportunity to share with others, and she knew in her heart that most of her guests wouldn't care that the table was adorned with palm and new linen, but she couldn't help herself. If it didn't look and smell and taste and sound perfect, she would never be able to relax.

She picked up her broom and began sweeping and tidying. She was running through her to-do list in her head as she worked and was so engrossed in what she was doing that she paid no attention to the noises outside. She didn't hear the young couple settling in for the night or the animals conveying their welcome in moos and clucks.

She continued working feverishly, and as she did, her busyness turned to frustration. Didn't anyone understand how important this was? Didn't anyone get it? Why was no one in her household taking it as seriously as she was? Why was no one down here, in the middle of the night, cleaning and tidying and decorating and setting? Wasn't her husband worried about what people would think if they came in and saw their inn not in tip-top shape? What if another inn had everything perfect and theirs was not? They had to be sure they kept up! As she mulled over her exasperation, she began sweeping more vigorously, and she became so intent on her work that she didn't pay any attention to the jug of water she had laid out for the next morning.

CRASH! She heard the loud sound the clay jar made as it hit the floor and shattered. Water and pieces of broken pottery flew across her floor, and she had to put her hand to her mouth to keep from screaming in frustration.

She looked around, sure she had woken the entire house. Thankfully, no one stirred. They must all be so exhausted from their travels that they didn't hear the crash. She was still irritated, but in this instance, she was glad she was alone in her work.

She bent down, cleaned up the pieces of broken clay, wiped up the water, and went to find another jar to fill with water. As she searched the cabinet, she became overwhelmed and began to sob, quietly so that she would not wake anyone in the house. What kind of hostess would she be if that happened?

She wanted so desperately to make everything perfect, and it just wasn't working out that way. The harder she worked, the more work there seemed to be. The house didn't look clean enough, the decorations not fancy enough, the table not perfect enough, the food not delicious enough. She simply wasn't going to be able to match the picture of perfection she had in her mind. She sat for a moment on the floor, her head in her hands, tears rolling down her cheeks and onto the floor beneath her.

She only allowed herself this short breakdown and then pulled herself together. She didn't have time for this. There was too much to do, and she was the only one who was going to do it and do it right. She grabbed the new jug and headed out the door toward the well next to the stable.

As she walked, she continued to run through the list of things she must get done before daybreak, when she heard voices coming from the stable. Who in the world would be in the stable with the animals in the middle of the night? Half fearful and half angry, she tiptoed toward the stable to investigate.

"Are you comfortable enough?" she heard a man's voice ask.

"Yes, Joseph, thank you. I am just fine. The innkeeper was kind and found us a blanket and some water. Now, please sit down," a young woman answered.

The innkeeper's wife peered through a crack in the stable wall and saw a young couple seated in the hay surrounded by the animals. The young man was fiddling with the straw, and as he stood up, the innkeeper's wife could see the young woman seated on the floor...she was pregnant! Very pregnant!

What in the world was a woman in her condition doing in their stable and lying on the floor? Surely her ears had deceived her, surely her husband had not purposefully brought this couple to their barn?!

What would people say? Oh, she dreaded the talk that would quickly spread in the morning when the town found out they sent a young, pregnant woman to sleep in their barn! Their reputation would be ruined, and she simply couldn't hold her tongue another minute.

She turned on her heel with every intention of storming off to the inn to give her husband a piece of her mind, but, right before she took a step, she heard the couple begin to speak again. She stepped closer to hear their conversation better and peered through a crack in the barn wall as she watched the young couple

"I am so sorry this is all I could find, Mary. You and the baby deserve a better place to rest for the night."

"Joseph," she answered him with a soothing smile, "don't be silly. This is wonderful. You found us a place to rest when we thought we would have nowhere. The hay is warm and soft, the animals are gentle, and I actually enjoy their company." She let out a soft giggle and ran her hand along the neck of the small donkey lying beside her.

The young woman's voice sent a feeling through the innkeeper's wife. It was as if she were drinking a warm honey that calmed and soothed her. She had heard hundreds, thousands, of voices in her time running this inn with her husband, and never had a voice struck her as this one did.

"This stable is warm, dry, and lovely. We are here together, and we are safe. That makes it perfect in my eyes."

The young man stepped forward and kissed his wife on the forehead and they settled down together in quiet rest.

The innkeeper's wife stepped back quietly and sat by the well. How could this be? The stable was "perfect"? There were many things in the world that were perfect, and this stable was far from one of them. It was dirty and smelly, and there were no clean linens or fine blankets, and yet this young soon-to-be mother seemed not only content but joyful. She was happy just being still and quiet and in her husband's arms...even without any trappings. No grand dinner, no soft bed, no warm blankets, no decorations hanging in the eaves above their heads. This couple sat among animals on the cold ground, and yet they were satisfied.

She sat for what seemed like hours, just listening to the young couple laugh together, and the to-do list that had been overtaking her mind for days began to fade from her thoughts.

When was the last time she had sat quietly with her husband or her children and just enjoyed their laughter? When was the last time she completed her tasks and then went to be in her husband's arms rather than adding ten extra things she wanted to accomplish before heading to sleep?

As she stood and walked slowly back to the inn, she began to reconsider what she considered "perfect." Could it be that her family and her guests would feel more welcomed and loved by her attention and time rather than a perfectly plated dinner?

She walked into the inn, set the jar on the table, and walked slowly to her room. She passed the rug that had folded up on one end, she passed the tray of food for the next morning, she didn't double check to ensure every date was sitting just so, and she passed the table and did not scrutinize the candles or the palms she had placed there.

She simply walked to her room, listening to the quiet night. She opened the door and heard the soft breathing of her husband as he slept. For the first time in what seemed like years, she crawled in next to him, kissed him softly on the cheek, and closed her eyes. A peace poured over her as she drifted to sleep, the sound of quiet wind and soft laughter ringing in her ears.

Chapter 3
THE LITTLE BOY

The young boy scooped the last bit of food into the trough for the animals, threw the empty feed bag into the corner, and ran out into the night. He was so excited that his legs seemed to run ahead of him in a way that his body couldn't keep up.

He sprinted down the small dirt path and into the main street of his hometown, Bethlehem. He had always thought Bethlehem was a boring place to grow up. Nothing ever happened here and nothing exciting ever seemed to come to town, but this night was different.

Since the travelers had arrived, the town was all in a flurry, and he loved it. He saw the inns and taverns decorated with welcoming palm branches and linen curtains. He smelled fresh baked bread in every oven and heard stories from far-off places. He was so wrapped up in the excitement of the night that he didn't see the tall man walking toward him. He ran right into a new traveler he had never met before.

"Oh, I'm sorry," said the man with a laugh, and the young boy looked up into the stranger's face.

"Oh, I'm sorry, sir. I wasn't paying attention. I'm off to the town to see the new arrivals and hear their stories."

He was in such a rush that he ran right past the man and into the town without even catching his name or seeing where he was going. How could he be expected to welcome a stranger when there were so many fun things to do?

Usually, the evenings in Bethlehem were quiet and dull but lately, there was just as much to see and do at night as in the day. The guests were talking and eating, the travelers were sharing stories, and the ladies of the town were busy keeping up with the demand for food and supplies.

This was the most exciting time he had ever experienced, and he wanted to see everything. He was just about out of earshot of the traveler when he heard him call out, "Excuse me, boy, but can you tell me where I could find some food for myself and my wife?"

The boy didn't want to stop what he was doing to help this man, but he knew if word got back to his mother that he had snubbed an adult, he would be in for it at home. So, the boy stopped running, sighed, and walked back to the man. When he got closer, he could see that the man looked very tired. "Have you been traveling long?" the boy asked.

"Yes." The man sighed. "My wife is resting up the hill, and I am trying to find food for her."

The boy looked up the hill. He must have heard the man wrong because there was nothing up that hill except the innkeeper's stable.

"She's resting up there?" the boy asked in surprise as he pointed to the stable.

"Yes," the man answered slowly. He seemed embarrassed by the question, and the boy didn't dare push the issue further.

"Yes, there is a place right in the center of town where you can buy food and drink. They aren't usually there this time of night, but with all of the travelers they are serving people even now."

The man thanked the boy and headed into town. The boy started to run back to his exciting evening, but a sound stopped him. He turned and looked up the hill and heard what sounded like a woman crying. He turned to where the man had stood to ask him if everything was okay, but all he could see was the edge of his cloak as he turned the corner and down the next street. The boy turned to investigate himself and slowly walked up the hill and peered into the innkeeper's stable.

He saw a young girl lying on the ground, not much older than his big sister. The girl was very pregnant and seemed to be upset. The boy wasn't sure what to do. Should he fetch the man he'd just sent into town? Should he ask his mother to come help the girl?

As he was questioning himself, he heard the laughter from town shoot up the hill. He turned with a tug on his heart. Oh, he wanted to go be in the excitement of the city. This wouldn't ever happen again, and he was missing it. He wanted to leave, but something kept him looking at the girl. He could hear her saying something very softly, and he leaned in closer to hear what it was.

The girl was praying. At first, he thought he should leave. It wasn't right to listen in on the prayers of another, but then he heard just how soft and gentle her prayers were, and he wanted to hear more. He couldn't hear her exact words, but just the tone of her prayer made him want to sit still and listen.

As he listened, the noises of the city began to fade, and he began to focus just on the sound. His own heart seemed to join the words of the young girl's prayers. He stopped watching her and slowly looked up into the sky.

The stars this night were clearer than he had ever seen them, and there was an excitement in the air around him that outshone the excitement he had felt in the city. He wasn't sure how it was possible, but suddenly sitting on the ground looking at the stars and mouthing a quiet prayer seemed like the most exciting thing he had ever done.

He didn't want to go into town in that moment. He didn't want to do anything but sit there and be surrounded by the thrill of the night. His young heart wasn't quite sure what was going on, but he knew something special was happening.

He could feel a presence that he couldn't see, and he wanted to hold onto that feeling as long as he could. He listened for a long time and slowly began to get tired. He lay down in the grass and began to drift off to sleep. He could hear the buzzing excitement of the night, but it wasn't from the city as it had been before. Now it was from his own heart.

Chapter 4
THE OLD SHEPHERD

There it was again, the slamming doors, the loud laughter, the clanging of dishes. Wasn't anyone going to go to sleep down there?

The old shepherd glanced over his shoulder at the small town below the hill he sat on. He had been a shepherd in Bethlehem all his life and he had never seen the town in such a state. Since the census order, there seemed to be an explosion of hustle and bustle in this sleepy town, and he hated it.

The hill he sat on to tend his sheep was only about a mile outside of town and usually the nights were quiet and still. He could lie under the tree and see the stars and hear the wind blow. But the last few nights, the horrible noise of the day spilled over into the night.

He hated these crowds overrunning his small town. He liked to be left alone, probably a byproduct of years tending sheep all on his own. He liked sheep. They were predictable and boring, and he liked it that way. He liked that Bethlehem was usually quiet, and he did not like this new big city atmosphere that had come to town.

He knew it was only for a short time, but he didn't care. It made him grumpy and angry. He wanted people to stop talking to him, to stop bumping into him when he went into town. He wanted people to just calm down and go away. Didn't they understand that all of this was an imposition? He heard a loud crash and an even louder roar of laughter in the town below, and he rolled his eyes and crossed his arms.

This was ridiculous and he couldn't wait for it all to just be over. He didn't understand all these townspeople overjoyed with the newcomers and visitors. They might think it was a great time for Bethlehem, but he most certainly did not.

He settled in under the tree, looked out over his sleeping flock, and fumed. He was so angry he couldn't relax and certainly couldn't enjoy the night.

As he glared back over the town of Bethlehem, he heard another noise. This one wasn't like the crash he heard earlier. This was more like a rumble, like distant thunder. He looked up at the night sky, but there was no cloud in sight. It couldn't be a storm rolling in.

It's probably another raucous party destroying the quiet town below me, he thought as he hit the ground angrily with his fist. Then he heard the sound again, but it grew louder. He looked around and realized it was not coming from Bethlehem but from the sky.

He stood and looked heavenward, trying to see whatever storm might be causing the sound. As he looked up, studying the sky, the noise changed. The rumble faded into a melody. He stood in awe as his ears picked up on the most beautiful music he had ever heard. The sounds of the city were drowned out by this peaceful and joyful sound. He was so enthralled by the sound that he became almost entranced. Where was this music coming from? His heart begged it not to stop and his ears perked to hear its words.

"Gloria," he heard some voices sing, then suddenly, he saw it—a host of angels standing above him, singing praises to the sky.

He fell back with fear. How could this be? What was happening?

"Fear not," he heard a voice say.

He looked up to see a beautiful figure speaking to him in the softest, kindest voice he had ever heard. He was drawn to the sound and to the beautiful singing still going on behind it.

"I bring you good news of great joy," the voice continued. "Today in the town of David, a Savior has been born. You will find the baby wrapped in cloths and lying in a manger."

As soon as the messenger had finished speaking, the beautiful singing grew louder. The praises were sung in voices so clear and the beauty of the sight was so vibrant that the old shepherd could not tear his eyes away. He stood rooted to the spot as the music filled his soul.

Suddenly, the anger, the loneliness, the frustration that had been building up in his heart for decades began to melt away. The music was like a soothing medicine that healed the wound of isolation in an instant. The sound of the singing pierced his ears and ran down his heart and soul.

He stood there listening to their words of praise, and then as quickly as they had arrived, the host of angels was gone. At first the old shepherd was saddened by their departure.

"Please, come back," he yelled to the now empty sky.

He longed to hear the sweet music again but as he paused and listened for the rustling to return, he realized he heard nothing. Not only did he not hear the angels returning, but he also did not hear the sound of the city below him. He knew the sounds must be there, but suddenly his ears weren't straining in anger to hear them. His heart felt lighter and his soul free for the first time in years.

He couldn't believe what he had just seen and heard! Angels. Angels in Bethlehem!! They had come here, to the city of David, to deliver a message. The message!

He had been so distracted by the beauty of the sound that he had almost forgotten the words they had shared. A baby was being born that night. A baby who was a Savior? He didn't understand what that meant, but he didn't care.

He was so overcome with the joy of the sound of the angels that he knew he must find this child. He grabbed his staff and began running toward the town. He didn't know where the child would be, but he knew the music still singing to his heart would lead him there.

Chapter 5
MARY

Mary watched as Joseph stepped out of the stable where they were resting and headed outside to find something for them to eat.

As she listened for his footsteps, to ensure he was gone, she let out a small sigh. The small sigh morphed into a larger whimper and then into soft sobs. She was trying so hard to be strong, but her resolve was wearing thin. She reached down and felt the baby kicking inside her.

"Why me, God?" she wondered aloud between sobs. "Why me?"

She was thankful that the Lord had chosen her. She was humbled by His trust in her, and yet she was scared and tired and alone.

She'd heard what people said behind her back before she and Joseph left to come to Bethlehem. Everyone could see she was pregnant, and everyone knew she and Joseph had not yet married. She heard the whispers; she heard the sneering comments and the gasps of shock.

She had told her family what the angel had said to her and while they said they believed her, she could hear the doubt in their voices. She didn't blame them, of course; how could she? If she were hearing this story from another young girl, she would likely be skeptical too.

She thought back to the sound of her mother and father discussing her pregnancy the night she told them about Gabriel's visit. She could still hear her mother's crying and the worry in her father's voice. She was thankful for their continued love and support, but she knew she would never hear their voices the same way again. She knew she would always hear the doubt in their words when she spoke of her son.

She heard the sound of children playing outside in the busy Bethlehem streets. She remembered playing with her friends as a child and running along the streets of her hometown. She cried harder as she thought about the fact that she would never hear the voice of her best friend, Delia, ever again.

When the news about her pregnancy had spread through town, all of her friends' families had forbidden them from ever speaking to Mary again. She still heard their voices as they called out horrible names that were reserved for unfaithful women at her.

Her heart grieved as she realized the familiar sounds of her childhood were gone now. The comfort and ease of going to sleep with those sounds in her ears was never to occur again. Before her was the complete unknown.

She felt the baby kick in her womb again and as he did, she felt a stirring in her heart. Was it a voice? Was it her mind playing tricks on her? What was that sound? Was it really there or was she tired and imagining it?

Oh, it was definitely there, though, even if no one else could hear it. She knew she was hearing a voice meant just for her.

"Focus on what I think, Mary. Look to me for your comfort and your peace. The world will not give you that, only I can." This message filled her ears like a thundering drum and her entire body vibrated with the power of the words.

She bowed her head in reverence for the words she knew in her heart came straight from the Lord her God. Once again, she'd heard a message that no one would believe. How many girls her age hear an audible message from the Almighty that no one else can hear?

But this time, she didn't feel alone or scared by the message. Instead, she felt proud and blessed.

She suddenly knew that even without her childhood home or friends and even without her parents, she was never alone or without a home. Her God was speaking to her, her God was with her, and He would shelter her heart and her mind. She settled back onto the straw and closed her eyes. She spoke the words of the message over and over to herself and let the beauty of the sound rock her to sleep.

Chapter 6
JOSEPH

Joseph sat on a bed of hay, unable to sleep. His wife was resting next to him, and he watched as she breathed peacefully. He knew it wouldn't be long until the child was born, and he was glad she was resting before the hard work began.

As he watched her sleep, he felt a familiar feeling begin to well up inside of him.

"How could you let this happen?" he heard himself say quietly.

He thought about Mary, about the angel that had come to him, about the message he had received. God's son...God's own son was going to be born, and this is where they are going to welcome him? In a stable surrounded by animals?

He was Mary's husband; it was his job to provide for them and protect them, and here they were sleeping in a stable. There wasn't even a place to lay the baby once he arrived. There was no family there to assist them, no bed for Mary to lie on, and no friends to congratulate them on the new arrival.

He had failed. Joseph had failed her, he had failed his family, he had failed them all. Why hadn't they left earlier? Why hadn't he written ahead and arranged for a place to stay? How could he have let this happen? This was the most special time of their lives, and he messed it all up.

As he stewed in his own self-doubt, he felt Mary stir beside him. She woke with a start and grabbed his hand.

"What is it, Mary?" he asked in a mild panic.

"It is time," she said breathlessly.

Joseph's heart and mind began to race. *This can't be it; it can't be time.*

He was not ready, and he knew with a little more time he could make things right and give her and the child the birthplace they deserved. But as the next few hours passed, it became clear that this was in fact the time and there would be no correcting their location or situation.

The evening went by in a mixture of worry and doubt. Mary pushed and worked as she labored in childbirth, and Joseph tried his best to help her. He didn't know what to do, and he continued to kick himself for letting this event happen in these circumstances. He hated himself for letting Mary go through this alone and in a stable, and while she cried out in pain, all he could hear was the voice in his head telling him all of this was his fault.

If he had done better, she would be in a room surrounded by women who knew how to help her, and she wouldn't be in so much pain. The feelings of failure ran through his mind over and over and began to cloud out any other thought, sight, or sound.

Just as it seemed it would overtake him, a sound pierced through the fog. It was as if he were sleepwalking, and someone jarred him awake. He strained to hear the sound again. It was like a hand was extending to him, and if he could just hear it better, he could grab it and be pulled back into the present.

Then there it was again, and the dense self-doubt shot out of his mind as if a bright light had sent the darkness running. It was the cry of a baby.

Joseph looked down and there was Mary, holding Jesus and smiling. The cries of a newborn can often be ear splitting, yet Joseph stood mesmerized by this baby's cries. These cries were somehow soothing and comforting. It made no logical sense, and yet it was true; as Joseph heard the baby's cries he was empowered and stronger.

He looked at the child, and it seemed as if a light radiated from his face. The moment he looked into Jesus's eyes it was as if a booming voice could be heard in Joseph's ears.

"You are enough because I love you," a voice spoke to his heart.

Who was speaking? Joseph looked around and saw no one. The voice was so loud and so real that it seemed as if it must be coming from a person standing nearby, but there was no one there.

As Joseph stood and listened to the baby crying, he suddenly understood in a way that was indescribable. This baby, this baby would change everything.

Joseph didn't need to hear the voice telling him he wasn't good enough, because this baby had chosen him to be here in this moment. This baby's cries were like words Joseph could understand, telling him that he was enough, he was loved, and he had not failed at all.

His son, his earthly son was looking at him in a way that shattered his self-doubt. This baby was truly God. This baby had chosen Mary and had chosen him. He had never thought about it like that before. He, of course, believed that Mary was chosen, but now he realized he was as well.

This baby's cries were words spoken to him through his earthly son's heart straight to Joseph's. "I chose you. You are enough, and you are loved. This was my choosing, Joseph—this place, this stable, this night. This was my choice, this is my plan, this is my perfect entrance."

He hadn't messed up. He hadn't let his family down, and he hadn't missed this moment. Oh, he almost had, he had almost missed the beauty of it all as he sank deeper into his own despair and guilt, but now he was present again. He was here, mind, body, and soul, and this was a moment he would cherish in his heart forever.

Chapter 7
GABRIEL

It was done. The Lord had finally entered the world of his children.

Gabriel looked around him, and all he could see was darkness and pain and sin. Compared to the beauty of his home in the heavens, this place made his stomach churn. Gabriel still didn't quite understand why God had created this plan to save this fallen and sin-ridden world.

But he knew that the Father's will was always perfect, and he listened to it. When God had first told him the message He was to deliver to Mary, he was astonished.

"Please don't leave us, Lord," he had begged the Son as He sat at the right hand of His Father.

"I am not leaving you, Gabriel, but this is the only way to save my children. Don't you yet understand our deep and abiding love for them?"

"But they turn from you time and again, Lord. Stay with us. The enemy trolls down there; here you are protected by your armies."

"I do not need your armies, Gabriel, although I am pleased with your willingness. I must go down to earth, I must become a human child, I must serve my children, and Gabriel, they must kill me."

"No, Lord," Gabriel boomed in the throne room. "No, how can that be? You are almighty, three in one, they must not be allowed to look upon you, let alone harm you."

That was when the Father stood.

"Gabriel."

One word. One word was all it took. Gabriel knew that this was the plan, that he was simply to follow it and to trust in his Lord.

"Yes, my God. I am your servant. Tell me what you ask of me."

He was given instructions and messages to relay, and he began his journey to Mary. When he reached her, he instantly knew why she had been chosen for this task, although she did look rather young.

He watched her for a while, curious as to exactly what the Trinity had seen in her. The glow she gave off made it clear to any heavenly body that she was a special soul, but he wanted to know more. He remained with her all day as she prayed and worked and spoke with others. Her voice was soft and kind, her heart was the purest he had ever seen, and her prayers were like songs of worship floating on the air.

He had heard the words of wise Abraham, he had heard the commanding voice of Moses as he spoke to the Israelites, he had heard the sweet songs of David, and the trumpets at the walls of Jericho, and yet the prayers he heard leave the lips of this young girl set his heart on fire.

The prayers were meant for his God, but just hearing them on earth as she spoke them, they made his resolve all the greater that this was the plan of the Trinity and this was his mission.

It had been many months since he delivered that message, and he had stood by her side, invisible to her, for all that time. He could see the enemy prowling past her as she walked the streets of Bethlehem. He could see Satan's minions whisper vile and hate-filled insults into the ears of Mary's so-called community as they hurled the words at her and laughed. He saw the black fingers of the demons as they tried their best to grab for her and for Joseph, but he would not be moved. He had remained by Mary's side, protecting her, and comforting her all these months and now all this night.

He knew the Father wanted him to be on guard for the enemy, and that was exactly what he planned to do. He wished he could speak to Mary audibly in a way to comfort her cries of loneliness and pain, but he knew that only upon the call of the Father could he speak in a voice she could hear or appear in a form she could see.

So instead, he stood guard, invisible and silent to the humans all around him. As he peered into the faces of these humans, he knew he would never fully understand this world or its people, but there was one thing he did know, and that was the goodness of God.

He stood by Mary's side, engrossed in his mission of protection. He was so laser-focused on what was "out there" that he almost missed what had come in. He heard a sound and immediately had the feeling of being home in the heavens, but how was that possible? He knew he was on earth, and he knew this was far from the glory of the Lord's home.

He heard the sound again. It was a familiar sound, and yet in a way it was unfamiliar. He looked over and saw the sleeping baby in Mary's arms, and that was when he knew. He knew the voice in that cry, he knew the look of love in those eyes, he knew the sense of peace that flowed from that spirit. He knew this was God's son.

He had been told by the Father that this had been the plan all along, but somehow this sound shook him from knowing to truly seeing. He knew it was God's son because he had been told, but now he could truly see it because he recognized the Son.

He heard the whisper of God's voice every time the baby made a sound. Yes, it was the sound of a human baby, but for those who had stood before the Almighty and heard His voice, it was clear that His voice was in that baby's cry. He could hear Jesus, God the Father, and the Holy Spirit all in the single cry of this child.

This was it. His Lord was here on earth, in the body of that tiny infant.

He still didn't understand, and he knew it was not his place to question, and so he simply stood and listened. Listened to the beautiful and powerful breath of God in the cries of a baby.

Chapter 8
JESUS

Oh, He longed to ease their hearts and worries. He was here! He was here for them and yet they could not see His divinity, only his humanity.

He knew many would walk by Him in the next 33 years and most would only hear his human voice, but there would be those who would listen with their hearts and not their ears and would hear the message from the Almighty Father. Baby Jesus lay in Mary's arms and while he was all infant, he was also all God. He could hear the hearts and minds inside the inn.

He could hear the innkeeper fighting with his own heart, trying to focus on the sound of peace instead of the sound of the empty money bag. Jesus knew the innkeeper only wanted to serve, but he was missing the point of his life. It was wonderful that he wanted to help others, but he was so overcome with what he did not have to give, that he was forgetting what he did have. Jesus knew the desire for more would steal many hearts away from him.

He listened as the innkeeper's wife wrestled with her desire to be perfect in the eyes of those around her. He loved that she wished to make things beautiful; after all, He and the Father created beauty, but they also created love and family and closeness. She was so overcome by the need to please others that she was missing out on the beauty of relationships not only with those closest to her, but with God. He wished to draw her close and tell her that He saw her inner beauty, and she was His precious one.

He could hear the snoring of the little boy as he slept in the grass outside. He loved his child, and He asked the Holy Spirit to guide him as he grew. Jesus wanted the boy to see He had come for him, and this was what real excitement was all about. He was happy the little boy was enjoying himself and the life he had been given, but He longed for the little boy to take a moment and realize that the excitement and fun out there in the town, was nothing compared to the wonder that was going on right here in the stable. This is what it was really all about.

Jesus could hear the racing heart of the old shepherd as he ran towards the stable. He knew the shepherd was lonely and that it had hardened his heart. He knew that only God could heal past hurts and that only God could grant him peace and joy even in difficult times. He wanted to touch the poor old shepherd's hand and let him know that he was never alone. He wanted to ease his hurt and to show him that despite what the world had done to him, that he was a child of the Most High, and that he was important and loved and never forgotten.

Baby Jesus looked up at Joseph and heard the cries of his heart. Dear Joseph, who served God so faithfully and yet who carried so much self-doubt. Jesus wished Joseph could see himself as God saw him, loved and worthy and capable with God's help. He longed for Joseph to understand he was chosen, he was hand-picked for just this time, and just this moment. He had not messed up, he was not a failure; this was the plan all along, Joseph just was trying to push God's plan aside for his own. If only he could make Joseph see the perfection in this plan and that even if he had failed, which he would do throughout his human life, that he was still deeply loved. He smiled as he thought of the times He would have with Joseph in the years to come. This man would protect His human side, and in turn, Jesus would save him from himself.

Jesus snuggled closer to Mary, and as He did, he heard her heart beating. She carried such a burden in her mind, struggling between thankfulness for the job God had given her and sorrow for the life she was giving up. He knew his mother's heart was the purest He and the Father had ever seen, and yet He knew she was human and struggled to fight the enemy, who hated her more than anyone who had ever lived. His all-knowing heart ached to know the pain that she would feel as she watched Him on the cross. He would do all he could in the next 33 years to make her understand, but He had much work to do and all of His children needed Him. He would not have long in the soft caress of Mary's arms, and He knew He must comfort her with His presence in the time He had.

He looked up at the faithful Gabriel, and their eyes met. This heavenly messenger who had been God's servant with strength and purpose. He looked at Gabriel and could still see a rush of confusion on his face. He knew that no one but Himself, the Holy Spirit, and the Father truly understood this plan in its fullness, but He also knew that Gabriel would follow their call no matter what.

Jesus listened to the sounds around Him and the sounds of the world.

His human ears could hear the neighing of the horses, the rustling of the sheep, the slow breathing of his resting mother, and the sounds of the busy city outside the stable.

His eternal heart heard the world's voice. He heard the pain, the suffering, and the sorrow that had taken over His beautiful creation.

He knew the voices of doubt that were coming, the sound of the crowd screaming at Him. He could already hear the clang of the nail as it pierced His hands and the wailing of His mother as she looked on.

He knew what was before Him, and He chose it yet again, because in this quiet night He could also hear the praises of thanksgiving to those who would follow Him, accept Him, and join Him in the Heavens. He knew the sounds of this world and the sounds of this first Christmas and every Christmas that was to come, and He loved them all.

Epilogue
THE REAL SOUNDS OF CHRISTMAS

I woke up from my daydream with tears streaming down my face. My boys may have destroyed my nativity set, but they opened my eyes to the beauty of a story I had been too busy to take the time to really see. My heart beat faster as I looked at the broken pieces in the trash can. I was so much like these figures.

I was just like the innkeeper, overwhelmed with guilt each Christmas or birthday or holiday when I couldn't give my family all they asked for and desired. I know you shouldn't spoil your kids, but my heart wanted so badly to see their excited faces as they opened every gift on their list. But what was I teaching them and myself by seeking more and more and more? What small, everyday blessings were falling to the wayside because I was too busy searching for "more"? Christmas presents are fun. I still wanted to go wrap up a few surprises and place them under my tree for my family and friends, but I was now determined that this Christmas, I would focus more on the star at the top of my tree rather than the gifts below it.

I was just like the innkeeper's wife, always wanting to be perfect, to put my picture-perfect foot forward and losing my mind in the process. Even with this broken nativity set, was my first thought how grateful I am that my boys have the nativity set to see and to explore and to ask questions about, or was it that now I had an empty space in my decorations that looked unsightly? Beautiful things come from God, and I enjoy decorating my home for him and welcoming people to it; but I was determined that this Christmas my home would be more about Christ filling it, rather than decorations filling it.

I was just like the little boy, so caught up in the holiday movies, the parties, the Santa visits, the hustle and bustle, that I was forgetting what it was all really about. The parties were fun and I would still go and enjoy the concerts and the special events, but I was determined that this Christmas I would see the meaning of Christmas rather than the events of Christmas.

I was just like the old shepherd, cranky and frustrated that everything wasn't going my way. I loved the hustle and bustle, and yet it quickly became too much each and every year. Too many people in the grocery store, too many people at the mall, too much noise, and too much pressure. I found myself wanting it all to just pass quickly so my regular life could start back again in January. How had I lost the beauty and peace of this season? I knew that even with the best of intentions, the season and all of its trappings could become overwhelming, but I was determined that this Christmas, I would find the peace and joy rather than the pressure and frustration.

I was just like Joseph, overwhelmed with guilt that I continually fail. I'm not the mom I should be, I'm not the wife I want to be, I don't do my devotions regularly enough, my prayer life often falls to the side of my to-do list, there is not enough time, there are not enough healthy meals on my table, and it's all my fault. I want to be more than I was ever capable of being, and as I was honest with myself, I was trying to be more than I was ever meant to be here on this earth. These feelings of "not good enough" come from only one place, and that is the enemy. I stood there and thought about the deep love of God that He would come to earth for me, and I was determined that this Christmas I would give God the glory for the season, I would give Him my heart, and I would give the enemy back my guilt.

I was just like Mary, thankful but sorrowful. I know how blessed I am. I hear the three tornadoes raging above me and I know they are healthy and happy and I am blessed. But, I feel the sharp stick of longing too. I often see "the grass is greener on the other side" and I forget to focus on what I have right in front of me. I see others sitting in seats of power at lofty jobs, while I clean up spilt Cheerios. I see my friends all off to girls' weekends, while I was uninvited and feeling very lonely. I see the life I planned as a distant memory, and I fail to see how beautiful the life I have now is, and I am determined that this Christmas I will see my blessings rather than my heartaches.

I am even like Gabriel, confused by a plan that I don't quite understand. I know God has a plan and I know it is perfect, but when I look around the world I mostly see hurt and fear and hatred. Why doesn't God make the changes that seem to make sense to my human mind? But this Christmas I am determined to hear God's voice in everything around me and to focus on His voice rather than the voice of the world.

I stood up, trash bag in hand, listening to the sounds of Christmas in my own home—Bing Crosby crooning over the radio, the fire crackling in the fireplace, the cat scurrying to try to knock another ornament from the tree, my boys playing upstairs—and I am reminded of how easy it has always been to lose sight of the truth.

These figures were there, they saw it all happen, and yet they, too, struggled to find the real Christmas. Jesus has come. He is here among us every day. All we have to do is truly listen for the true sounds of Christmas, the knock on the door of our heart, the laughter of our loved ones, the prayers of our fellow believers, the praises of the choirs, the encouragement of the Lord's love, the blessings of His goodness, and the promises in His word. It's all there…all any of us have to do is listen for the real sounds of the season, the sounds that call us back to Him.

www.ingramcontent.com/pod-product-compliance
Lightning Source LLC
LaVergne TN
LVHW011900060526
838200LV00054B/4435